AF363210

NAN COOSEMANS & FLORIAN HIELE

Teenagers and the lockdown

7 steps to guide your child during and after this challenging time

YOUNITE EDIZIONI

www.youniteonline.com

Copyright © 2020 **Younite**
All rights reserved.

No part of this book may be used or reproduced
without the authors' prior and written permission.

1st edition **June 2020**

Title | Teenagers and the lockdown: 7 steps to guide your
child during and after this challenging time

Authors | Nan Coosemans e Florian Hiele

ISBN: 9788894538434

Content

PART ONE

- Who we are and why we wrote this book
- Why it is so important to safeguard teenagers
- How teenagers experience the lockdown: the results from our survey on 1000 teenagers

PART TWO

Foreword: Shifting your perspective on the lockdown

 # 1st step: At home...Dealing with your emotions and theirs, the smart way
- What can you as a parent do in order to transform your teenager's behavior into growth opportunities?

 # 2nd step: Taking good care the body and mind for the sake of both sides
- The 4 personality styles of children; how to motivate them to do all kinds of activities

 # 3rd step: Working as a team and building a routine that suits everyone
- How to get your teenagers to respect you

 # 4th step: Treating your children as problem solving partners
- How to negotiate with teenagers without quarreling
- Download the free video from our website

 # 5th step – Helping your children look ahead
- Smart listening makes a happier environment

 # 6th step – Remember that you are always their parent!

 # 7th step – Their growth process continues after the end of the lockdown

PART ONE

Who we are and why we wrote this book

Dear parent,
let's start by introducing ourselves: we are *Florian Hiele and Nan Coosemans, Family Coaches e Youth Trainers.*

We are Dutch-born but have been living for some years now in Italy, where we founded *the first online school for parents with pre-adolescent and adolescent children*, ranging from 8 to 18 years old! (currently available in Italian only).

Besides my involvement with the online school, I, Nan, am also the author of the book *"Quello che i ragazzi non dicono"* ("What teens don't tell you"; this, too, currently available in Italian only) and together we are the founders of **Younite®**, *a training company for families and youths*, we organize international summer camps in Italy, the Netherlands and Ibiza for teenagers to work on their self-esteem, goals and awareness, give trainings into schools, seminars and coaching one to one with teens and families. In 2018

"What teens don't tell you": the book that gives teenagers a voice and enables parents to understand their children better.

Understanding and interpreting teenage silences. Published by Sperling & Kupfer.

we started **YADA** (Youth awareness development Academy) a training company to become Family Coach or Youth Trainer.
At the end of this opening chapter you can find two paragraphs entirely about us so that – if you want – you can get to know us better (who we are, where we studied and what else we do). What matters to us now is to tell you **why we decided to write**

this book in no time and made sure it has a huge outreach by selling it at such a great price.

Here in Italy we are living a very tough situation, which, unfortunately and very gradually, is replicating the world over with more or less the same pattern.
Teenagers and their parents are our foremost concern and safeguarding both in this extremely challenging situation has become our mission.

We soon realized that **no advice can be found on how to safeguard teenagers** during the lockdown.
In Italy we tackled the problem by giving a series of free webinars, but even **at international level we noticed that no one took the time to talk about teenagers and how to deal with them in the current situation!**

As experts in the teenage world as well as family coaches **we want to show parents – in 7 easy steps – how to live the lockdown** peacefully **with their family and how to guide their teenagers during and after the lockdown.**

We feel that this situation is challenging enough and thus, without the proper amount of attention and awareness, it can easily become traumatic for both adults and teenagers.

We should all learn how to behave at home, now during the lockdown as well as later when we will have to accept the new reality in which we will be living, made of precise rules and (for some more time) of limitations.
In these 7 steps **we unravel what is going on in the mind of yure teenager** now and **how you**, as a parent, **can best react** to turn this into a constructive moment.

Part of the content of this book is based on the very recent findings of a **survey carried out during the past month** on a **sample of 1000 teenagers** throughout Italy.

Why is it so important to safeguard teenagers?
Teenagers face a very critical phase of their life: they are forced to leave behind them the body and mind they had as children and to start wearing a new and adult body with a brand new mind.

In order to prepare them for this change, their body activates a series of hormones that affect their mood, their emotions, and their psychological state. **Teenagers** feel trapped in the identity they had up to a short while ago, **but have no clue yet about who they will become and have a hard time discovering it.**
It's the age in which they have the urge to go out, make experiences, discover who they are, distance themselves from their parents, open up with their friends, test their physical, emotional and intellectual ability.

What do you think goes on inside their head when all of a sudden they find themselves in the midst of the most turbulent time of their life and are forced to stay at home, afraid of everything that is going on, totally distressed for not knowing when this will all be over while being deprived of a space of their own where they can let go of the pressure?
You can clearly understand by yourself that this is a very challenging moment for them and that **now more than ever they extremely need you to understand and guide them.**

That's it! They need a **role model** (trust us, you are theirs, though it may not seem like it) **to live the lockdown happily**, to accept the restrictions imposed on them, to develop flexibility, patience and resilience and feel **emotionally more stable**. They need these skills both to face the present and to accept a future which, as already said, will keep setting new rules.

Teenagers see themselves undergoing a great stress and **if you don't learn to read the signs of this stress you might risk**

underestimating their emotions, you could get mad at them and quarrel, you could even decide to punish them instead of understanding that they are simply asking for your help.

You can turn this period into a constructive one for you and your children or into the worst one of your life: it's up to you.

What we can tell you is that **by following these 7 easy steps you are giving yourself and your family the opportunity to come out of this situation stronger than ever before.**

Yes, because the good news is that even though, as we said before, teenagers are going through a delicate phase, they are also highly resourceful and if you manage to spur and motivate them properly, you will see that they can even think of this period as fun.

You don't believe us? Go ahead and read the findings from our survey!

Enjoy reading. We wish you a good lockdown and post lockdown!

@ Photo: Alessandro Annunziata

How teenagers experience the lockdown: the findings from our survey on 1000 teenagers

As we mentioned before, this month we carried out a **survey on 1000 teenagers in Italy.**

In this survey **we asked the teenagers what were the pros and cons of the lockdown** and some of the answers were quite unexpected.

CONS

What was the most negative part of the lockdown for you?
(Respondents 1000 teenagers age 10-21)
- Not seeing my friends
- Not going out
- Always feeling lonely
- Not being able to do sports
- Missing my family
- Missing my freedom
- Video lessons
- Anxiety issues/ not being able to sleep
- Being bored
- Not being able to see my boyfriend / my girlfriend
- Not being able to stay outdoors

FINDINGS
- Teenagers miss having new physical experiences
- It's easy for teenagers to lock themselves away in a world of their own with their phone
- They suffer from not being able to live real life situations
- Communicating only virtually with their friends is tough
- They miss getting real school grades and wonder

whether they will be able to make it to the next class
- They miss a "place" (where they won't feel judged) in which to let go of their emotions and stress

PROS

What was the most positive thing for you during the lockdown? *(Respondents 1000 teenagers age 10-21 years)*
- Devoting more time to my hobbies
- Devoting more time to myself
- Spending more time with my family
- Not going to school and lessons taught on computer
- Knowing that pollution has gone way down
- Netflix
- Getting more sleep
- Re-evaluating my priorities
- Learning to cook
- Getting more rest
- Discovering new hobbies
- Eating a lot

FINDINGS
- Teenagers are available for more introspection
- They appreciate having more time with their family
- They have profound thoughts about the world
- They feel less stressed

Here is a chart that shows which are the strongest emotions that the 1000 teenagers we surveyed are feeling at this time.

When answering: **Which emotion recurred more often during this period?** 44,7% of teenagers said "boredom" (this is not a negative result, believe us!); 28,6% said "frustration" and only 14% "anxiety".

WHICH EMOTION RECURRED
MORE OFTEN DURING THIS PERIOD?

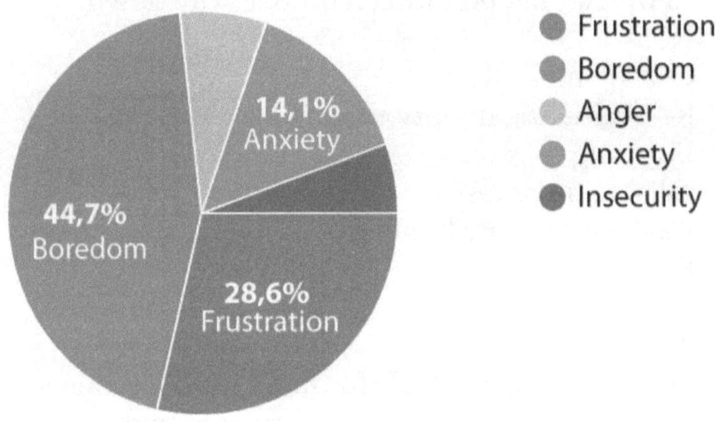

As you have read, **even teenagers recognize the upsides of this experience** and we can assure you that the way they live at home during this time can be very relatable to their answers, making them more positive or more negative.

PART TWO

Foreword: Shifting your perspective on the lockdown

Before starting the 7 easy steps we ask you to make a very important change of mindset.
The first thing we suggest is to shift your perspective on this moment shifting from a pessimistic equation to an optimistic one (it has already been said that happiness is a very simple equation…).

The shift that we suggest is the following:
from -> **lockdown** = boredom, stress, forced cohabitation, getting upset, doubled workload, continuous efforts, small house, I don't have a garden, I feel oppressed;

to -> **lockdown** = unique moment that will never come back (we truly hope so!) to rethink what matters to you and to your family, to reestablish family values, to get to know your children better and become a better parent.

In our normal everyday life we are always in a hurry, always busy, always time starved in every situation. We become parents and from that moment on we start living in a commitment vortex that sucks us into it. We meet our children at lunchtime or at dinnertime directly home from work (especially if they are teenagers and are always hanging around).

We would love to have quiet family moment, we would really love – for once – to feel closer or to be able to share moments of only "fun" only and of zero "duties".

Well, we have them now and we can make them become precious moments. So off to work and let's see how to live this situation at home in the best possible way preserving everyone's wellbeing.

How can you transform the lockdown into a moment of growth?

We can show you in our 7 easy steps, let's see them straight away!

 # 1st STEP – AT HOME...DEALING WITH YOUR EMOTIONS AND THEIRS, THE SMART WAY

@ Photo: Andrea Piacquadio

The 1st Step is the most important one of all because it all starts from here.

In this period of isolation **everything that they see at home is their world right now,** even if they absorb information from YouTube or other platforms, the most important information is the one they absorb at home.

Right now your role as a parent is much more important, almost more important than before.

The way you deal with your emotions and you interact with them is what matters most. Don't forget that **even if they don't want to listen to you, their mirror neurons are always very active.**

This is why you every day should ask yourself: **how can I be a good example? What example have I been so far during this time?** How am I stimulating my children? Have I been very negative? Have I complained too much? Have I always been mad? **How have I been talking about these days to them and my partner while at home?**

Look at these days as a gym so that you can understand where you can work out more.

@ Photo: Stefano Giorgetti

What does "dealing with emotions the smart way" mean?

When we ask you to deal with your emotions, and your children's as well, **we don't mean** that you should suppress all negative emotions and **force yourself to be happy**, always being chirpy with them while something else is going on inside.

What we suggest is to deal **with your negative emotions in a different way,** channeling their power into something constructive and - **most of all - sharing this process with your children.**

Let's see together how.

1) Share your inner process with your children.

It means that you can show yourself bored, frustrated, stressed, sad, gloomy or anything else. What a relief! You don't have to fake anything. What we advise you, though, is **to show your children how you are able – all by yourself – to find a solution to this mindset by being proactive.**

The main issue is to **teach your children that external situations can be difficult to deal with, but we always have the freedom to choose how we react.** If you think of it, it's true… none of us has any power over what goes on outside, but **we all have full and total control over what goes on inside of us.**

@ Photo: Alessandro Annunziata

2) Don't try to find solutions for your children's moods.

There are plenty of activities that can't be done at home right now and your children feel deprived of the things they care about most: **going out with their friends, staying outdoors and grabbing bits of independence away from your control.**

It's so easy for strong emotions to well up inside. Anger, boredom and frustration are the most common and – we're talking about teenagers – the reaction will probably be either one of the 2 most common ones:

- Blaming their emotions on you or other family members
- Denying their emotions because they don't want to seem vulnerable or because they don't know how to handle them

@ Photo: Alessandro Annunziata

What can you as a parent do in order to transform your teenager's behavior into growth opportunities?

1) Do not suppress any emotion, allow yourself and your children to welcome negative emotions as you would welcome positive emotions.

2) Take responsibility for your emotions and teach your children to do so as well. This means: don't try to step in in finding a solution to their anxiety or anger!

3) Activate smart communication to avoid fights, in step no. 2 we will explain smart communication.

4) Show interest and ask them how they are even when their "crisis" seems over. Remember that you don't have to control them, just show genuine interest.

During these days in lockdown it's important for your children to realize that **you are fully aware of their emotions** and understand them, but that **it's up to them to find a solution to their emotional crisis.**

Here's a practical example.

Your teenager comes to you and say: "Mom/Dad, I am SO bored! Staying here is such a drag!". What can you do? **Don't give them the solution outright**, like "Play a game of Monopoly, chat with your friends, read that book". Rather, try to ask them a question: "What could you do to not be bored? I know it would be great to go outside, I'm really fed up, too, today but I'm sure that we can find something to do". This way you show your child that you are also empathic and that you know how to deal with boredom.

Speaking about boredom, we would also like to tell you that **boring moments are great moments of growth for your children.** We'll discuss this more in depth later, but let's just mention that when kids fling themselves on the couch because they can't stay on the phone or play video games, or watch TV their **brain finally really activates itself** and they **start pondering** about themselves, nurturing new ideas and having important thoughts about themselves and others.

We hope you found this first step helpful, let's move on to the next STEP!

@ *Photo: Alessandro Annunziata*

 # 2nd STEP – TAKING GOOD CARE OF THE BODY AND MIND FOR THE SAKE OF BOTH SIDES

@ *Photo: Gustavo Fring*

We bet that you've already been told 1000 times that working out and eating healthy enables you to get the most physical and mental benefits but now the time has come to give these words a different meaning and really take them seriously!

We're not kidding; parents are the first who need to get serious about training their body and eating healthy if they are concerned about their family's wellbeing.

We're not talking about becoming fitness addicted, but about **taking at least 30 minutes a day to exercise**, do stretching, or work out any way you want.

It's extremely important to keep a close eye on your diet **avoiding sugary foods and drinks as well as junk food that also have a negative effect on the mind.** What we always tell teenagers is that their body is like a scooter, if you put gasoline in it but it has a diesel engine, you won't go anywhere!

Think about it, we have been given too many restrictions: less activity, less light, less outdoor time for those who do not have a balcony, less space.

What kind of space are we talking about?

Physical space and emotional space, meaning that we have less space to stay with our emotions, to express them, to let them out, to make them go away.

Think about anger; how many times did you get mad and then went out of the house, met a friend, went running or took a walk and then you got over it?

Now both you and your children cannot do it and **you as parent cannot allow your house to become a time bomb** because this would damage your relationship with your teenager and would have long-term consequences.

Now think how great it would be to be able to say the following: I am getting along with my son/daughter, we have found a way of living together, we are doing ok even if the world is in trouble, my house is in harmony.

Right now a home is like a lake without inlets or outlets...it can easily become a pond!

So what's in a pond? A proliferation of bacteria, slime and

diseases. Do you want this to take place in your mind or in your children's? Do you want them to become ponds?

We don't think so; if you're here it's exactly because you don't want this to happen!

Then go put your sneakers and trainers on and get going, you can find everything you need online. **Convey the message to your children that, in order to face this situation, you need to work out and eat healthy.**

Your children will absorb this stimulus like sponges, don't worry if they won't start right away, if you follow the other 5 steps of this e-book you also will learn to speak to them calmly and to persuade them.

To understand the importance of sports, **you should also know that kids have an extreme need for new experiences because that's how they produce the dopamine** they need to stay well and to overcome the down moments and the sharp changes caused by hormones at their age.

They produce dopamine when they are with their friends, having fun with their boy or girlfriend, when they can go on outings by themselves, when they practice their favorite sports!

How can we get them to produce dopamine at home, when every day is the same?

Well, on one hand they can find a solution by themselves and they do it via their phone, which for the is the outside world (we'll talk about their phone very soon), on the other hand **it's sport that helps us create dopamine: dancing, treadmill, hitting a heavy bag, lifting weights.**

Everything works and everything helps in keeping the level of dopamine high, yours and theirs (and they need it more than you do!).

Going back to the phone… it's important for you to understand two things: first is that if you set very tight rules on its use, now is the time to loosen them a bit because the phone is such a huge component of their school and social world. The second is that is remains highly inconvenient to let **your kids go to bed with their phones.**

@ Photo: John-Matk Smith

Important studies show how phones create disorders in our physical and mental system, so it is vital to put it offline at least one hour before going to bed.

This is why we suggest you negotiate a special arrangement with your children: more phone time during the day and no phone before going to bed (at least 1 hour) except for rare cases or emergencies. If kids want to use their phone to watch a movie or do their evening homework, make sure that the apps

that can block social media are active, so that your children can turn off the outer world and fully live the here and now.

You can help your children to set their phone momentarily aside by creating shared moments in the evening, like watching a movie together, cooking something delicious and then tasting it all together as well as any other activity that comes to your mind. **Did you know that teenagers tend to go to bed late because their body has a delayed production of melatonin?** That's why they have a hard time falling asleep and waking up early.

Many parents are complaining that their children lock themselves in their rooms, isolating themselves even more than before. The irony of it all… We are isolated and they seek further isolation! lol.
We try to joke about it but in these cases it's vital to urge them to respect a few rules, like eating all together at mealtime, doing sports and sharing some moments of social interaction at home.

How can you persuade your teenage kids without getting into a fight? We'll explain it in the next paragraph.

Avoid or reduce conflicts at home by using smart communication.

These days you are forced to live together and the risk that any conversation may turn into a fight is incredibly high. You can avoid this by learning to communicate the smart way.

When speaking to your children try to follow these 6 rules very carefully and you'll see that in a few days you will obtain miraculous results:

1) Connect to the frequency of their emotion.

Observe your children: are they angry? Sorry? Scared? Bored? Behave likewise: are they hyperactive? Talk fast. Are they sad? Talk more slowly and in a lower voice. Try to have the right posture; if they are scared you can't look too domineering, it would be intimidating.

@ Photo: Cottombro

2) Listen to your children to understand them and not to be understood.

Tell us the truth: when your children are talking, are you racing ahead thinking what to answer? Are you already thinking what you would like to tell or ask them? If the answer is yes, you had better try to avoid this approach and learn to listen in order to understand. If your children talk to you it's because they need you, so try not to make them regret it.

3) Say "I", you do not hold the truth.

Instead of saying "you must do some sports, it will make you feel better", try giving your opinion: "I think that doing some sports is a great idea because we are spending so much time inside at home and sports help us stay positive". Even when speaking of your emotions, always say "I"; never say "you upset me", say "I'm upset".

4) Let your children see your vulnerability.

If you are bored, if you are frustrated express this frustration (in a responsible manner, without putting the blame on others). Teach your children that every human being is vulnerable but that vulnerable doesn't mean weak. It will be a lesson for a ifetime. and being like that does not make us weak.

5) Find the right moment to speak.

If you must tell your children something, try to find the right moment. Try to understand that when they are feeling a very intense and maybe negative emotion may not be the right moment for a conversation. You can take up the discussion again when things have calmed down and a very good timing is before they go to bed. They are calmer, more emotional and open to sharing something with you.

6) Give them time.

Maybe you don't know it but teenagers require more time to process all the information and emotions because their brain has a different structure from ours. Don't expect an immediate reaction to everything you say. You can't pull the grass to make it grow faster!

The 4 personality styles in children and how to motivate them to do any kind of activity.

Did you know that a lot has been written about 4 major personality styles in children?

Each style has its characteristics and it is vital that you as a parent are able to recognize them so that you can motivate your children.

We bet you can't wait to find out what style relates to your children. First, though, we would like to explain why they often rebel when they are asked to do something.

You need to know that it's not a matter of lack of motivation or being lazy, it's just that they are motivated to do what's important for them.

Furthermore, the lack of motivation is a form of resistance. **If your children don't want to do something,** they can only express their power by resisting, because often they don't even have the freedom to do things their own way.

How can you understand how to react to this behavior and stimulate motivation?

It depends what your children's structure is.

Let's see together the 4 different personality styles created by Jennifer Nacif, a Mexican trainer, coach and leader.

@ *Photo: AbsolutVision*

PATIENT

Patient children are friendly and understanding. Good listeners, good at team work, they love harmony and need **safety.**

This is the key to their motivation: give them safety. If you want your patient child to do something it's important for you to use a reassuring tone of voice, it's important for you to be kind and peaceful in making your request.

For example: if your child is stressed by something you can be reassuring and say "ok, we can look at this together, I can help you find the right kind of training for you or we can find a quiet place where you can study".

SOCIAL

Social children are emotional people, they love to talk and connect with others, they are charismatic and popular. Children with this personality need to connect with others so if you want to motivate them you need to give them fun and connection.

For example: you can ask your child to do sports live on FB with a friend, to set up a private group on social media to work out all together every day! A social child will love this idea. You could also suggest a TikTok sports challenge.

ANALYTICAL

Analytical children are **perfectionists**, generally more mature than their age, courteous, rigid and all they want is clarity.

Here is how you can motivate them: promising clarity in exchange of something else. Be clear about you do, what you expect of them and respect the rules that you have

negotiated no matter what because children with this personality are uncompromising and they will break any deal should they believe a behavior to be disrespectful.

For example: to a child with this personality you can say: "can I help you out in dealing with this situation? Can I help you out lay out a plan for all the pages you have to study?"

DOMINANT

Dominant children are very demanding, they want to control everything, they are daring and quick and very responsible. Children with this personality love challenges because by nature they are problem solvers.

For them it is very important to have power, so you can leave them the power to manage to manage certain issues on their own as a way of motivating them to take action. With children of this personality you have even less chances of being successful if you tell them "go do your homework straight away". It won't work! You have to motivate them by making them feel powerful.

For example: you could say: "darling, I don't how to do this thing, could you help me out?" or " You know what you could do? You could organize a training schedule for all of us here at home and then we'll discuss it with the others".
You must know that your children could fit in more than one category, but it's up to you to single out their dominant style.

Once you find the right communication for your children's style, you will be able to motivate them because you will be adapting to their nature!

To be sure to motivate your children you must simply know

them: what personality do they have? What do they really want? What kind of questions do the ask themselves? What are their goals and ambitions?

You don't have to make them do 50 different things, but you must make them the things that fit their nature best. You'll see how they will be motivated! Now you have all the time you want to discover everything about your children.

Let's give another example: if, when you talk with your children you realize they are visual, meaning that they learn best with videos, you can suggest them to study on YouTube, too, and look for videos related to that subject and show them. One thing is for sure: they'll learn 30 times faster!

@ Photo: Julia M Cameron

9 tips to motivate them with their homework

Don't fight over homework, it doesn't work, if your children don't want to do their homework try to understand why

- Stay in touch with their teachers and find out what kind of teachers they have because some of them could be – for your children – very boring – while others could be very fun
- Make sure they have a quiet space, well lit and with a good workstation where they can be comfortable
- Encourage your children to ask their teacher and classmates for help, don't do it for them, but urge them to do it and advise them on how they could communicate with a teacher or a classmate
- Set a routine, a time for lessons, a time for homework, you don't have to do these things for them but you must guide them because they don't know how to manage their time and how to be organized
- Encourage them to take also long breaks, maybe you can prepare a snack, you can allow them to play at the PlayStation, do a TikTok, listen to some music
- Make sure that your children know that you are really there if they have a problem. This point is incredibly important because letting them grow up doesn't mean vanishing from their sight, but being there for them in another mode

@ *Photo: Alessandro Annunziata*

3rd STEP – WORKING AS A TEAM AND BUILDING A ROUTINE THAT SUITS EVERYONE

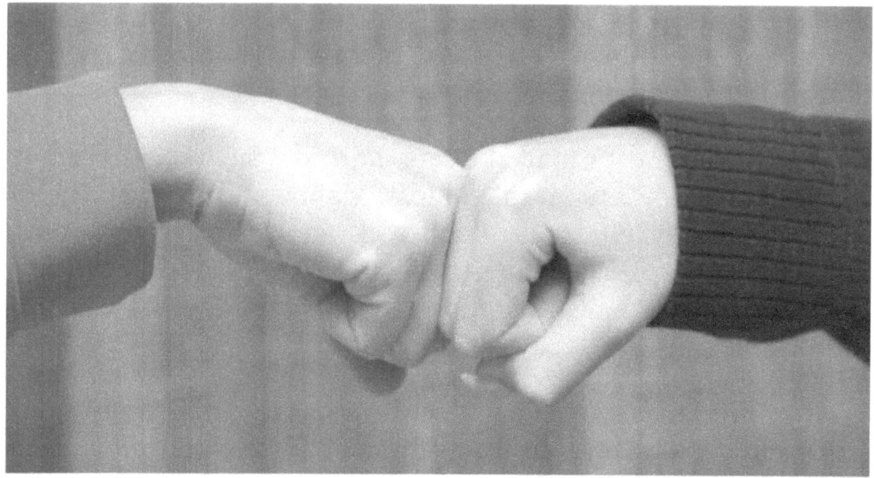

Family doesn't mean just being under the same roof, a warm meal or money when needed.

It is vital for our kids to learn at home what they are not taught in school. We often send our children to school believing that they will be able to learn everything there, but it isn't so. Home is where they are able to learn many other skills that are fundamental in life, such as teamwork.

A family is like a small company; members all have tasks, roles and skills of their own. As **a parent you can create a weekly or daily routine custom made for your family.**

For example you can decide that during the week the alarm goes off early because there are the online school lessons, while on weekends everyone can get more sleep. You can keep breakfast as a shared moment; you can create a slot in the afternoon for homework only and an evening one for movies, board games or anything else.

It's important for your children to sense that there is a roadmap no matter what, even if its pace and schedule are more relaxed.

Routine is important because "after" we will go back to a normal (o semi-normal) life and there still will be schedules that need to be respected.

Besides, we are human beings and as such we need a routine if we don't want to feel lost. Maybe at the beginning of the lockdown it felt good to be free from schedules and being able to do as we pleased, but in order to face a long lockdown and post lockdown in a healthy and productive manner it is so very important to stick to a clear routine.

We recommend that you decide this routine with your children without forcing upon them activities that may seem productive to you but they don't like.

If during the lockdown everyone is cooking, it might not be what your children want to do. In deciding the family routine, make sure that you give your children total freedom of choice for their spare time.

There are no activities more productive than others that "must" be done. Forget the word "must" and use "want" instead. There is no better recreational activity than the one that your children like best.

In this routine remember to include also moments of physical absence.

We're talking about some alone time, even if you are all un-der the same roof. Make sure that each family member, which means you too! can isolate a bit, staying by him/herself and enjoy just plain doing nothing. In the beginning your children may complain about these empty moments, but we assure you that these moments will be extremely important for them.

As a matter of fact, the lockdown has given us the opportunity to own our time again and to get back in touch with boredom and just plain doing nothing.

@ Photo: Alessandro Annunziata

A moment that should not seem wasted but – on the contrary – has the hidden potential of allowing you and your children to explore your inner world and understand what you really want, how you feel. In other words, in these empty moments each of you will learn a lot about him/herself.

If your children say they are bored, don't run for cover suggesting thousands of distractions or worrying about their irritation. Smile, instead, and help them understand that moments like that must be accepted and that they (by themselves) can find a solution to their mood.

Going back to our routine, it's important to add that once the schedule has been set **the rules previously negotiated must be respected.**

If you don't know how to be respected and how to re-establish your leadership within your family, here are our tips.

First rule (PLEASE memorize it!!!): "you cannot teach respect to your teenagers"

@ Photo: Alessandro Annunziata

Yes, you heard us right, we are telling you the opposite of what you usually read in books and articles: you cannot teach respect, **you can only show it to your children.**

There is no other method that is sure to work besides your example.

This is why the earlier you stop repeating to yourself that "you must teach your children respect" and you start repeating the "you must show your children respect" instead, the earlier you reach the desired goal.

In order to understand how to show your children respect, start asking yourself a very important question: **what does respect mean to me?** (here below you will find some blank lines where you can write your answer).

Usually, when we ask parents this question, many answer that "respect" to them means "not shouting", "not offending", "helping out at home", "obeying without arguing", etc.

And what is respect for you?

We ask you to take a few minutes to answer and to **list a series of practical actions that – in your view – could explain the meaning of "Respect".**

RESPECT

a feeling that leads us to recognize the
rights and dignity of someone or something

What does Respect mean to me?

Now that you have the definition of "respect", we'd like to ask you: **Do you do what is on your list?**

Do you always speak gently and calmly to you partner, to your children, to your family? Do you always answer nicely, even when you are having a bad day?

If the answer is "yes", then go on reading and understanding what you can do to get your children to respect you. If the answer is "no", then we advise you not to forget that respect starts from you and if you want to keep your parental leadership you can start working on yourself.

@ Photo: Sabina Paci

YOUNITE, TRAINING COMPANY FOR FAMILIES AND TEENAGERS

Avoid the most common mistake and discover what to do when your children don't respect you.

The mistake that most parents do is to **take their children's aggressive reactions personally** and so, every time their kids misbehave, they start pointing their fingers at them and accuse them of being disrespectful.

Actually, very often teenagers have thousands of reasons for being nervous, but they simply don't know how to express their emotions so they blame their parents or siblings shouting and being offensive or slamming their door and isolating themselves.

So, first of all, avoid being hyper reactive and when your children lack respect, **force yourself** to stop, think it over and **ask them if something is wrong.**

You have no idea of the incredible effect that this change of attitude can produce. By so doing you reach two goals:

- you show your children that you are worried about them and you care to know if something is troubling them

- you manage to stay in your sphere of influence and to control yourself instead of controlling them.

4th STEP - TREATING YOUR CHILDREN AS PROBLEM SOLVING PARTNERS

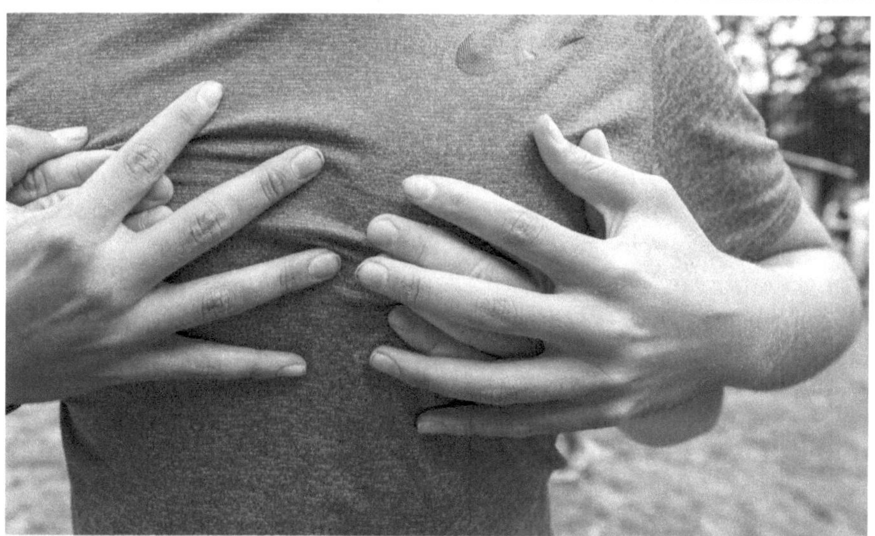

@ Photo: Alessandro Annunziata

As a parent of teenage children right now you are playing the role of the guide, you are no longer their teacher, like when they were little and you had to teach them to do everything; you are now a guide, a coach.

This said, dealing with the problems that this situation is creating, if your children were little, you could be the one to find solutions to make their life better, but **since your children are teenagers, the right way to act is to involve them in finding solutions.**

We always ask parents: what kind of children do you want? Children who do as you say or children who think with their own head and are capable of finding solutions?
Make it a habit to lay out all problems on the table and find their solution with your children.
For example, **if you realize that your children are spending**

way too much time with their phones, you can call them calmly and tell them: "we are forced to stay home and this is leading you to use you phone too much. I realize that your phone is important for you but for your wellbeing it's also important to find moments away from your phones so how can we manage? I would say that you could spend 3 hours on the phone each day. What do you say?"

It's absolutely normal for your children to answer: "What do you want? It's not your business! Leave us alone!" and it's important that – at that precise moment – instead of getting mad, you start a negotiation by asking: "how many hours would you like to be on the phone?"

This is the way to raise responsible, independent and self-reliant children: by teaching them to negotiate, that's one thing they'll never learn in school and they must learn it from you!

If you always force everything on your teenage children, you will only harm them, you won't help them grow and face this moment in a mature way. Not only that, you will get the opposite by showing that you are not respecting them.

The fact is that teenagers are in that phase of their life in which they need to understand whether they will succeed in becoming adults or not and you are the one who can give them validation. If you treat them as small children, forcing things upon them, you are sending them the following message: "you are not able to decide on your own and to take care of yourself".

Don't worry if they can't find a solution, later you will. The important thing is that you've included them in the decision making process.

Download the video course "Emotional Intelligence with teenagers", guide your teen in how to cope with their emotions on our website: *https://www.youniteonline.com/freeresources*

5th STEP – HELPING YOUR CHILDREN LOOK AHEAD

A way of making your children be well in times like these is to try to shift their current thoughts towards a future that will come true. Behind every negative thought of today lies a wish that your children are not yet aware of and still have to discover.

If, for example, one day your children really feel discouraged, lock themselves in their room and say they are blue, behind those emotions there is most certainly a desire. Your job as a

parent is to understand what desire their negative feelings are connected to and then shift their thoughts towards the desire they are currently manifesting as anger and sadness.

Very often parents say: "yes, I understand why you got mad" whereas they actually have no idea why their children are really mad. Maybe they have only a vague idea but without investigating they won't be able to find out what desire that emotion is connected to.

The moment you see your children having negative emotions, if they are willing to talk, ask them why they feel that way and what is really bothering them.

Only if you manage to discover this information can you reassure them giving them the answers they need like, for example: "I am sure that you'll go back doing lots of really cool stuff with your friends, that it'll be as exciting as ever before. I am absolutely positive that there will be a way to make up for all the trainings you missed with your team!".

You will notice an immediate change in your children because instead of just saying "I'm sorry, I understand you, what a difficult situation" you will manage to understand what they really want and desire and will also reassure them that soon they'll manage to have back the things they like. And even if they go on being upset, you can be sure that this technique will bring a smile back sooner than you think.

It's essential that when you listen to your children you do it without judging them and without judging their emotions because each emotion needs to be pulled out, otherwise it stays inside and creates a tense environment.

Furthermore, **when you help your children overcome this**

emotion, it is ever so important that you don't take any extreme reaction personally.

Bear in mind that they could be very angry and blame it on you. If you manage to overcome this moment, knowing that it has nothing to do with you, you can then get the answers that you

@ Photo: Alessandro Annunziata

need to help them. The emotion is theirs, not yours. Let them be angry, sad and frustrated, because that's the way their inner pressure goes down.

Remember step 1: you set the example; don't be hyper reactive and place yourself in a position of **smart listening**.

If you don't know how to do it, keep reading.

Make the family atmosphere calmer by practicing smart listening.

Those who study emotional intelligence, like we did for many years, know what an important practice smart listening is! **Teenagers whose parents are capable of listening to them** are calmer and happier because they know they can express their emotions at home and that there they will always find someone capable of understanding them without judging.

In a time like this it is paramount for your children to be sure that they are listened to, so we would like to guide you to the practice of smart listening by listing, once again, the steps you need to follow:

1) Make and keep eye contact all the while you are listening. For 2 main reasons: the first is that you are proving them that you are there and that you have time for them, the second is that just by looking into their eyes you can understand many of the things they need to tell you. Furthermore, with your eyes you can also convey your feelings; your children will understand that you are really interested and that you are calm.

2) Show genuine interest. Don't watch TV while they are talking to you, don't read the paper or scroll down pages on your phone, don't chop vegetables. Stop, what's the rush anyway? You have nowhere else to go, we are all locked down ;-). Stop and give them time. If you have something to do and you cannot delay your commitments, then ask them if you can talk about it later and decide together when.

3) Just listen. We're not kidding. Don't ask questions until your children aren't done talking. Don't interrupt, because this takes their attention away from what they were meaning to say and shows that you are in a hurry to end the conversation. Give them the time they need to express their thoughts and to reword them if necessary. This will enable them to think straight.

4) Make your questions at the end, few and open. Don't question them but lead them to questioning themselves. Asking open questions you won't make them feel that you only want to control the situation but will make them understand that you are there to support them in THEIR thought processes. Their opinion matters and you should always value it.

5) Always repeat what they said to check if you understood what they meant to say. This way not only will you be sure you understood your children, but you will give them solid proof that you were paying attention to their words and that you care to listen.

@ Photo: Alessandro Annunziata

Don't empathize with their emotions

Don't let your children's sadness become yours; don't let their gloom become yours. Your children are not missing out on the best times of their lives. They are facing a difficult and challenging time, there's no doubt about that, but you can a lot to make this become a joyful time as well.

Don't forget that now is the time you can let the very best part of you come through and turn yourself into a stronger, more resilient, more flexible and optimistic person.

Many parents wrote us saying: "Poor kids, they are missing the best part of their life!".

We would like to remind you that this situation will end and your children will live their lives happily. Each new experience in their life is always an experience and, thus, a moment of growth, which certainly does not harm them.

We would like to quote what a 15-year-old girl shared about this moment of lockdown:

"I think I'll appreciate freedom a lot more. Even the simple fact of being able to go out to do anything will be a lot nicer because you really appreciate things when you lose them. I think this is a real lesson to understand the value of what we have without taking anything for granted."

So don't be afraid if they are losing some moments because at the same time they are enriching themselves with life experiences.

6th STEP – REMEMBER THAT YOU ARE ALWAYS THEIR PARENT

When we say that you are always their parent we mean **that you are the person facing this challenge** and remember that **you have the ability to do so.**

You have already faced entirely new challenges for which you had to create the rules and understand how to behave, don't you remember?

The challenge of having social media is entirely new, it is unprecedented in history and you are creating new rules and are learning new ways to raise your children. You didn't grow up with a phone of your own, like us. This situation is something new for everyone and there has never been anything like it before! It's a phase that needs to be understood, managed and in which to grow learning something new!

If you must re-establish some rules, do so and create brand new ones. You are their guide and if you face challenges right now it doesn't mean there is something wrong with you, it's only a signal that there is something you need to learn to do better.

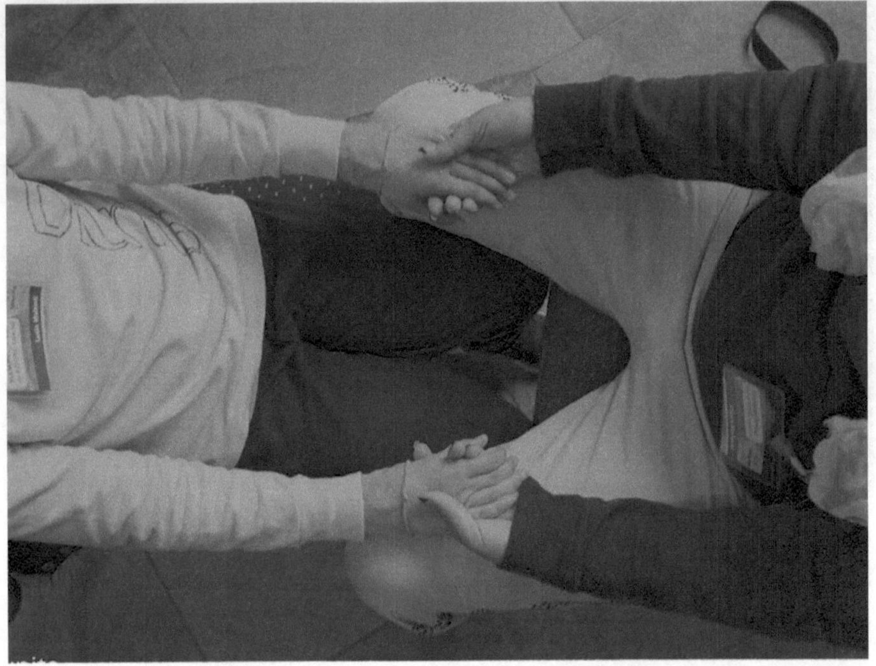

@ Photo: Alessandro Annunziata

For example, in this moment of forced cohabitation you might realize that your children don't respect you, that you are not good at dealing with emotions, that you are not able to understand their behaviors.

This moment of total shutdown forces us to see and live with parts of ourselves that can make us feel sometimes uncomfortable. But this not feeling comfortable can be extremely useful if you understand that it's actually a good sign because it shows you what and where you can

improve as a parent.
Keep being the parent and hold on to your rules. Even if you see your children bored and discouraged don't give up; don't change your rules.

Before we advised that it's best if kids don't go to bed with their phones. Make them respect this rule and if they say they're bored, let them be bored!
As we mentioned at the beginning of this e-book, our brain is much more creative when it has nothing to do. We realize it may seem a paradox, but it's true, **when our brain is still it can finally expand its abilities and create.**

If you want your children to make good use of their free time in the lockdown then let them also get bored. To prove that boredom is an ally of creativity just think that recent studies have shown how our brain's ability to learn increases when we take a break from what we are learning.

For example, let's suppose that your children are studying math and their brain is learning 75%, if they were to free their brain taking a break and return to their books after a while, their learning ability could go up to 85%.

When we tell you to stand firm in your role as a parent and in your rules, we are not saying that you shouldn't be sensitive and flexible towards their emotions.

It's true that you have to come up with new rules, but you should do so respecting the new situation. It's only natural for your children to be more bored, feel more sadness or anger right now and it's only natural that they may feel the need to spend more time on the phone or to eat more (their low level of dopamine increases their sweet tooth).

So, if before this time certain things were not allowed, you can create new rules keeping these new needs in mind. Don't make the mistake of diminishing your children's problems; don't ridicule them when they talk to you. Rather, listen to them and guide them in solving their problems without trading roles with them.

And remember ;-) there is no such thing as a perfect parent, but it is important to keep growing and – mostly – to take action using the tools that today are available.

7th STEP – THEIR GROWTH PROCESS CONTINUES AFTER THE END OF THE LOCKDOWN

@ Photo: Congerdesign

Before starting with the last step we want to show you the answer that teenagers gave to the question: "What's the first thing you will do once you are able to go out from the LOCKDOWN?"

- **Go out with friends**
- **See my whole family**
- **Go visit my grandmother / Hug my grandparents**
- **Hug everyone**
- **Race to the beautician**
- **See my girlfriend**
- **Spend the evening with my gang**
- **Go to the beach with my dog**

As you can see, it's very important for them to go out and discover, stay with others, have physical contact. So, if now you are worried that they won't go back to leading a normal life, don't be, because as soon as it will be possible teenagers will rush back to doing all these wonderful things.

In order to face the post lockdown in the best possible way, it's important for you now to concentrate on **looking at the future with awareness,** trying to be updated on everything your government determines. Don't stay glued to the TV screen, constantly watching minor shows or news broadcasts, but stay connected with the official information sources coming directly from the government.

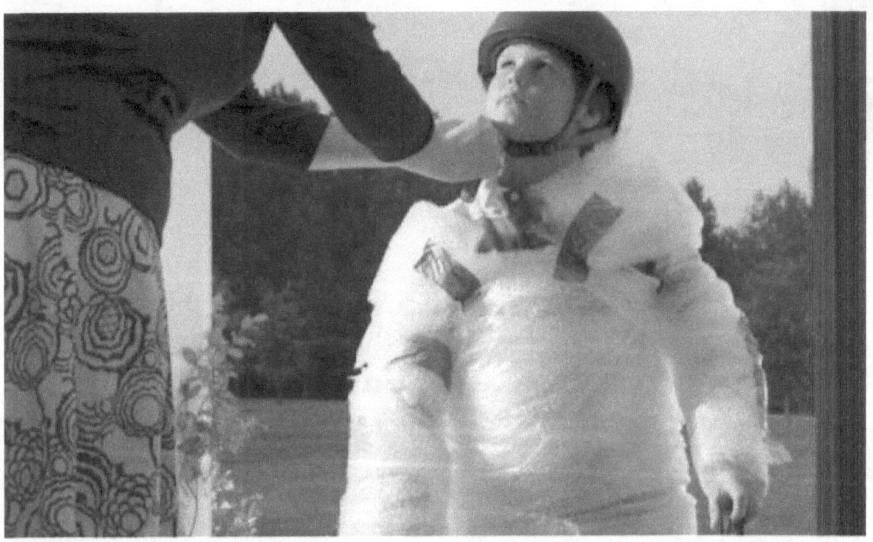

Why are we telling you this? Because if you keep giving your children rules based on what you think and not on what the governments says, and your rules are much stricter that the government's, there's a chance that your teenage children won't listen to you anymore.

Obviously, if their grandparents live at home with you, you can't give your children all the freedom that kids who don't live with elderly people have. In this case it's important for you to explain clearly and calmly to your children that you would love them to have this freedom but for now you must unfortunately abide by the law.

It's very important for you to be aligned with your partner concerning what rules to apply in the future to manage your family during the post lockdown. Your children must not be aware that there is different approach on either parent's side, but they must be guided in the same direction.
Once the rules have been decided you must obviously establish the consequences if these rules are not respected.

Another great thing you can do now is to **define with the whole family how you would you're your life to be once this moment is over**. You could realize that maybe afterwards you won't want to change many things and you might want to keep them going afterwards.

Don't miss this precious opportunity, **make a list of all the positive aspects that this period has given you and decide to make them become a habit even afterwards.**

Look at the post lockdown period as one of further growth and not only as going back to your old reality but – instead – as going back to a new reality where everyone has learned and experimented something new.

Once this situation will be over maybe many of your family values will have changed. Maybe now you are living in an apartment without a balcony in the center of the city and you realize that in the future you would love to go live in the country and have a big garden. Or you have always lived in the

country without really appreciating its advantages and now you all agree on how wonderful it is to have a bit of greenery just for you.

This situation is a transformative experience, let it take your family a new step forward.

Obviously in deciding what to keep and what to let go from this period it will be great to involve your children, too, and ask them what they liked and disliked about it. **Then create moments in which the whole family discusses this experience and make a note of what come out.**

Never impose your decision because, as we already mentioned, in raising a teenager you have to give up on the idea of imposing and giving orders. Instead, you should embrace the approach of involving them in the decision making process.

@ Photo: Alessandro Annunziata

How should you behave with your kids once they will be able to go out?

There are boys and girls who simply can't wait to go out and there are boys and girls who will be anxious because they may be afraid. Others won't want to go around with a face mask because it embarrasses them. Start understanding that each of these scenarios is possible and try to define how you as a parent could react.

For example, if your children are afraid, encourage them telling them that eating healthy and doing sports can raise their immune system and make them stronger. Point out that we all are much stronger than we believe.

It's important for you to reassure your children also because our nervous system is divided into two parts: sympathetic nervous system and parasympathetic nervous system, which is connected to our immune system.
When we are stressed, maybe because we are afraid, our parasympathetic system shuts off. When we live in anxiety and fear our immune system is less strong.
No wonder that your children, if terrified, could also recreate the symptoms of an illness, which they obviously don't actually have.

If your children belong to that category of kids who can't wait to go out and do all those things that were now forbidden, you should find a way to speak to then and make them understand that they must respect the rules also out of respect towards others who are weaker and more at risk.

A bit at a time we will all come out of this life changing "experience".

Don't worry and always remember that being a parent implies a constant growth and transformation: from the moment you knew you were expecting or when you learned you were going to be a father… it lasts a lifetime.

Being a parent is not easy because you are always revealing and testing yourself, but please also know that you have within you all the resources you need to do it at your very best.

We wish you and your children a wonderful evolution!

Florian Hiele & Nan Coosemans

YOUNITE, TRAINING COMPANY FOR FAMILIES AND TEENAGERS

NOTES

Who is Nan Coosemans

@ Photo: Alessandro Annunziata

Founder of **Younite®**, Trainer, researcher, Family and Youth Coach, **author of the book "Quello che i ragazzi non dicono"** ("What teens don't' tell you") published by Sperling & Kupfer and mother of 3 boys.

Nan has over 20 years of experience in the world of personal development and in 2010 she founded Younite®, a training company for youths and families and in 2016 Genitori in Azione, the first online school for parents of teenagers.

She studied several years in the USA, The Netherlands and the UK. **Together with the team from Younite® she has worked with thousands of teenagers and their families in The Netherlands and Italy.**
She is co-founder of the YADA academy, the first training school in Italy for Youth Trainers and Family Coaches.

Who is Florian Hiele

@ *Photo: Alessandro Annunziata*

Founder of **YADA,** speaker, writer, and researcher. He was introduced to the world of personal development at the age of 17.

After overcoming his social anxiety and depression, his life mission became putting teenagers in contact with personal development. He has successfully coached hundreds of clients (both adults and teenagers).

He studied in Europe and in the USA in multiple fields: psychology, human behavior and learning behaviors. He has PNL, EE, TLT and VT certifications, specializes in phobias and social anxieties and over 13 years of experience in teaching and training teenagers internationally.

Co-founder of Younite®, Founder of YADA, Founder of Sociale Vrijheid.

@ Photo: Alessandro Annunziata

YOUNITE, TRAINING COMPANY FOR FAMILIES AND TEENAGERS

Free Video Course

EMOTIONAL INTELLIGENCE WITH TEENAGERS

Guide your teen in how to cope with their emotions

www.youniteonline.com/freeresources

www.youniteonline.com

We are aware that this book cannot provide an answer to all of our children's questions and to their evolution (and to ours as parents, as well)!

Furthermore, today it is unthinkable to write a book or manual without the follow-up of a supporting website.
On our website you can find a lot of useful free contents: articles, e-books, video courses. You can also find information on all our courses: summer camps for teenagers, workshop for families.

We are happy to welcome you on:
https://www.youniteonline.com 

Facebook

Official Fanpage YOUNITE:
https://www.facebook.com/youniteonline/

Instagram

Official Younite page dedicated to teenagers:
https://instagram.com/youniteonline
Official Younite Family page dedicated to parents:
https://instagram.com/younitefamily

Cover Photo | Cottombro
Copywriter | Rossella Particco
Translation | Beatrice Orlandini
Pubblication | BOOKNESS
Project Coordinator | Letizia Colombani

ISBN: 9788894538434

www.youniteonline.com

If you want to know all the latest news and activities,
subscribe to our mailing list.
Keep in touch and stay updated!